THE TAO OF DADDYING

Ancient Wisdom for Modern Fathers

By
Gregory Sporleder

Gregorysporleder.com

Cover Design by Heng Swee Lim
www.ilovedoodle.com

Dedication

I dedicate this book to my Mom and Dad, Bev and Jim Sporleder, who were the perfect examples of wise parenting. And of course to my wonderful wife Meghan, who made me a father by bringing both Ruby and Bodhi into this crazy world. But really, it's dedicated to them, Ruby Adeline and Bodhi James, who allow me the honor of trying my hardest to be a Wise Daddy

Introduction

I was standing in one of those gigantic bookstores—you know the one, helping my two toddlers spread the plethora of books they had chosen to peruse across the tiny table, getting them settled in for a little "booky-booky" time, as we called it back then. My kids and I alternated between the library and this bookstore, sometimes on a daily basis, because we didn't watch TV at our house, or at least the kids didn't. My wife, who had turned an art project into a multi-million-dollar clothing business, and all the pain and glory that entails, loved TV, and once the kids were asleep, she'd watch a little, then read, then pass out, but not before praying everyone would stay asleep for at least six or seven hours, before it started all over again. During baseball season, I watched until my team was eliminated, then lay in bed staring at the ceiling, wondering how I was going to keep my marriage alive, kids thriving, clean the garage—while pursuing my Hollywood acting career.

No TV for the kids made it tough—most toddlers watch a ton of it—but my wife and I were determined to keep the precious minds of our little angels free for as long as possible from the hypnosis that is television. It was especially hard to explain to my four-year-old, hands on her hips, staring at the blank screen, wishing whoever this Elmo character she kept hearing about would appear and explain to her why Daddy tries to be an actor on TV, but she and her little brother couldn't watch any.

"When you're older" I would say. Older came at ten, and now they won't stop watching—but that's for another book.

Between my wifes business and trying to stay awake during auditions, and with no other families living near us, the stress and pressure built. Eventually, we came face to face with the reality that raising these two toddlers was going to be the hardest and most important thing we would ever do. So, we made an executive decision: I would become a Stay-At-Home Daddy.

I committed to the job for four years straight.

Which brings us back to the huge bookstore. Once the kids where settled into booky-booky time, I would get coffee and look for books myself, mostly parenting books, because I didn't want to fall behind in my work skill set. I would often stand in the parenting book section and think, Geez, they didn't have any of this when my Mom and Dad were parenting, and I considered them some of the best parents ever. But I kept reading, certain there was more I needed to learn, adding to the shelf of all the other parenting books I owned.

Well, it just so happens....

Across from that bookshelf sits a small altar, with a big, beautifully carved wooden Buddha my sister had given me. Scattered around the Buddha were postcards, candles, precious rocks, shells, feathers, and other magic trinkets. And leaning against the Buddha was the most magic object of all: Stephen Mitchell's translation of the *Tao Te Ching*.

Next to this altar was my favorite St. Vincent de Paul thrift-shop chair, which my wife had refused to allow in the bedroom, She voted for the garage, and we compromised on the office. It was in this magic chair that Daddy took his well-earned time outs and read the Tao.

There wasn't an exact moment, but, eventually I realized that the Tao, which had changed my life in my late twenties, contained all the wisdom I needed to raise my kids. It had helped me see the world in a new and beautiful way, and to feel connected not only to myself but to the entire universe. The Tao had taught me to see the glory and purpose of almost anything and everything. It reminded me to laugh, love, and play, and that death, a natural part of life, wasn't far off. And, if you allowed the wisdom of these 81 poems to permeate your life, you would find contentment. Slowly but surely, I stopped buying parenting books. Everything I needed was right there in the Tao.

It worked. Every day I took the kids outside, where things made so much more sense. Whether it was the park, trail, beach, or just the backyard, we played outside with our friend Nature. The wisdom of the Tao showed itself daily.

Even though my kids are teenagers now (yet another book, maybe two) and I've gone back to work, I still sit in my magic chair and read the Tao. And it's still encouraging me to do my best.

About a year ago I was walking my dogs I saw a young Daddy struggling, his kid was having park meltdown. The Daddy and the kid looked like he could use a little encouragement so I went over and helped. Used my dogs to break the ice and within a few minutes, Voila. The Daddy smiled, said thanks, and I thought, Wait, don't thank me, thank the Tao.

And that's how the idea for this book was born.

I feel wholeheartedly that if Lao-Tzu magically appeared and read what I have written, he would approve. Because this book, like his, was written to encourage. So, on that note....

Daddy on, Wise Daddies.

GS

A Brief History of the Tao

The Tao is an ancient Chinese philosophy that was written in the late 4th century BCE (before Christ area) by a guy named Lao Lzu. legend has it that old Lao Tzu, who's name, translated, means Old boy or Old master, apparently was fed up with the moral decay of human society and he decided to head up into the mountains to live as a hermit. He got to the western gate of the kingdom where a young sentry asked the old timer if he would write down all his wisdom before he left. What Lao Tzu left behind is believed to be the Tao Te Ching, which translated means the book of the way, or the book of the way of virtue. Only the Bible has been translated more than Lao Tzu's 81 poems.

I would also like to acknowledge that I referenced many translations of the Tao but always returned to Stephen Mitchell's, whose version serves as my treasure map to contentment.

1

The Tao of Daddying cannot be told.
Words do it little justice.
Action is proof of its existence.

Words were created to describe the mystery.
The job of a Wise Daddy is to bring
the mystery to life.
Don't base your Daddying on words
but on actions.

Yet, words and actions arise
from the same source,
Love.

Loving to love,
this is the way to love them forever.

2

There is the sleeping child
and there is the tantrum.
There are smiles,
there are tears.

With this in mind
the Wise Daddy stays calm,
commits to his actions,
making sure they are worthy.
Things arise, he is there,
things disappear, he is there.
He shows power through kindness.
When he finally sleeps,
he lets everything go,
knowing that tomorrow is not far off.

Sometimes he snores.
So he is told.

3

If you brag,
your Kids head will swell,
give them too much stuff,
they won't understand worth.
The Wise Daddy leads with action.
He does things worth watching.
By giving them more of your time,
they need fewer things.

The Wise Daddy knows their friends
and is aware of all,
the good and the questionable.
He protects but doesn't judge.
He allows his Kid to figure out
who is who.
Be open with your Kids
and your Kids will open to you.

4

The Tao is like a good nap
on a soft couch
in a quiet space.
The Wise Daddy understands this.
Simple yet priceless,
worthy, yet difficult to attain.
It's there for you
when you need it,
and even when you don't.
I don't know where the Tao came from,
but like a good nap
I'm grateful it exists.

5

The Tao doesn't play favorites.
It gives birth to both girls and boys.
The Wise Daddy doesn't prefer.
Boy and Girl help each other,
define each other,
follow each other,
need each other.
Girls and Boys create each other.

The Wise Daddy plays.
Girl or Boy,
both are good.
The more fun you have,
the more love is generated.
And when fun becomes love,
it's impossible to explain.
A Wise Daddy
is always ready
to play.

6

The Tao is considered the Great Mother.
This is no coincidence.
Know the magic of mothering.
Find the Mother in you.
She's in there,
utilize her wisdom
to your best ability.

Being a Wise Daddy is boundless, never-ending.
Why is it boundless?
The first time you hold them
a new world begins.
Why is it never-ending?
Because love is eternal.

The Wise Daddy's love
Is beyond his emotions.
He is able to do
whatever needs doing.
Because he commits,
he is completely fulfilled.

8

The Wise Daddy is like water,
it is essential to living
and cleans the dirty.
They both stay humble and low.
This makes them like the Tao.

Help the Kids tend their space.
Teach them to think.
When fighting erupts, be fair and generous.
In deciding, explain and don't be bossy.

Do your work with them in mind.
Wherever possible, create fun.
Allow yourself to become yourself.
Let others be themselves.
Why compare or compete?
Contented, you will be both
loved and respected.

9

Yelling, they become deaf.
Buying more stuff
won't make them love you more.
Care too much about other parents' opinions,
your Kid won't recognize you.
Fill the bowl to the brim,
you're asking for a mess.
Stay open, be nice,
and the crown is yours.

10

Can you stay focused
and reap the benefits?
Can you make time to exercise
so you can truly play with your Kid?
Can you reveal Nature to them
and show your love for It?
Without forcing them,
can you get them to follow you?

Make the effort to truly communicate
with the Feminine.
Let decisions take their course.
Step back from a tantrum
and see the bigger picture.
They are here, and they are hungry.
They are yours,
yet they belong to the world.

Find your humility.
Show them the way to themselves.
This is the mission.
The Tao is on your side.

11

When the line is crossed,
a Wise Daddy starts by listening.
He then judges fairly
explaining his decision.
Done explaining,
he hands out the terms
and sticks by them vehemently.

It is hard to discipline,
but it must be done.
Properly.

12

Too much media warps the mind.
Make sure the music's not too loud.
Healthy food is essential.
One way or another, find meditation.
Wanting everything is unrealistic.
The Wise Daddy stays alert,
trusts himself
and the Tao.
He lets things happen.
He is ready for anything.

13

A happy kid is as vulnerable as an unhappy one.
Hovering over them is self-indulgent.
What does it mean,
"A happy kid is as vulnerable as an unhappy kid?"
Regardless of where they stand in the moment,
they are yours for life.
They need you.

What does
"Hovering over them is self-indulgent" mean?
Hovering smothers them
and serves only the hoverer.
Allow them their freedom
That's how they learn to fly.
See yourself in them.
Encourage the best to emerge.

Loving them helps us love ourselves,
then we can care for all things.

14

Even with all the words in the world,
the Tao is indescribable.
You can't know the Tao,
but you can be the Tao.
Wise Daddies are proof.

It's impossible to see when the TV is on,
impossible to hear with music blaring.
impossible to reach with busy hands.
When we allow the Tao
to be part of our Daddying
we realize it's been there
forever.
The Tao simply reminds us
of the way things should be.

Look inside,
the Tao will be looking back.

15

Wise Daddies are calm, cool-headed,
their patience unfathomable,
their inner workings mysterious.
It is far easier to describe their actions.

They are as careful as a Kid lighting
his first firecracker,
alert as a lifeguard at a toddler pool party,
courteous as a visiting Grandma,
fluid as melting ice cream,
flexible as new Play-Doh,
ready to play, open for fun,
untroubled by trouble.

Do you have the patience to let your Kid
make pancakes?
Can you stand by and let them make a mess,
while smiling?
The Wise Daddy believes in his Kid,
He allows them to grow into themselves.
He's always ready to eat,
always ready to help clean up.

16

Each of us belongs in this world.
Breathing makes it so.
Recognizing our breathing is serenity.
When you discover the ruckus is a pillow fight
can you just watch and breathe,
allowing them to duke it out
knowing they will eventually
run out of breath?

When we lose touch with our breathing,
we tense up, choke.
When we tune into our breathing,
we are reminded that we are alive
and have the potential to be as loving,
helpful, nice, and respectful
as we can possibly be.
Immersed in the joy of breathing,
it is easy to stay connected to the Tao,
and when death arrives,
our last breath will be sweet.

17

When the Wise Daddy is in charge
the Kids play
and learn as they play.
Next best, is the Daddy who leads with words.
Next, the one that yells.
Worst is the Daddy that is mean.
Violent Daddies should be jailed.

Kids don't want to be forced,
so don't force.
The Wise Daddy allows them to play
and plays along,
and when it's time to go back inside,
the Kids go.

18

When we deny the Tao,
Daddies must bribe and manipulate.
When the Daddy doesn't provide enough exercise,
the Kid gets lazy, unhealthy.
If the Daddy can't find his primal instinct,
the family learns from external forces.

When the Daddy doesn't evolve,
the family becomes stuck.
Don't let this happen,
allow the Tao.

19

As nicely as possible,
turn off the technology.
Get out the games, old and new.
Make things.
Glue is magic, if you let it.
Bake a cake,
build a hide-out,
perform a show,
stage a parade,
use what you have.
They will eventually find the right balance.

When all else fails,
go outside.
Fun was born outside.

The Wise Daddy makes certain
to protect and nurture
his Kids imagination.

20

Stop worrying.
Sometimes it's yes, sometimes it's no.
Stop envying others.
Do they really have it better than you?
Stand tall, breathe deeply, regardless.
Others seem overly prepared and efficient,
running their families like a drill sergeant.
The Good Daddy convinces his Kid,
"We work together,
your job is as important as mine."

Others seem to have so much.
The Wise Daddy teaches moderation.
"We think before we buy,
we use the things we have.
Everything has its purpose."
Others treat food differently than the Wise Daddy.
He teaches his Kid,
"Eat good food,
take what you will eat, enjoy it."

☯

Food is precious,
the fuel for thinking and exercise.
Be grateful for it.
The Wise Daddy is different
from ordinary Daddies.
His rules and regulations are drawn
from Nature.
Nature is his real boss.
He strives to please Her.

21

The Tao is incomprehensible.
The Tao is mysterious.
The Wise Daddy keeps the Tao always in mind.
It keeps him sane.

How does he keep it in mind?
He constantly reminds himself,
"I am the Tao."
How does it keep him sane?
He allows it to.
The Tao created sanity.
The Wise Daddy doesn't bother
trying to understand why,
He's simply grateful
to have found it,
right there,
where it's always been
from the very beginning,
inside himself.

22

☯

If you want them to be happier,
help them with their sadness.
If you want them to be stronger,
exercise together.
If you want them to be smarter,
become smarter yourself.
If you want them to start something new,
start something new with them.
If you want them to have more,
show them how to give more.

By living in the Tao, the Wise Daddy
becomes a role model.
Because he is humble,
his Kid learns from him.
Because he speaks wisdom,
his Kid listens to him.
Because he is giving,
his Kid loves to give.
Because he cares for all,
his Kid loves him.
Be the Tao,
be yourself.

23

Administer discipline,
then keep quiet.
As in nature,
the pup must be reminded of its place.
At the same time
the leader of the pack
knows the pup must grow
and one day lead.

It's not easy to discipline.
But when we discipline from the Tao,
it makes sense to all.
Be fair and honest,
and it won't come back to bite you.
This is the natural order of things.
Find and believe in your primal instinct.
Wise Daddies have relied on it
since the beginning
of time.

24

When you go to work,
be sure to come home.
Time well managed
is worth time and a half.
Work with your Kid in mind
and time will fly.

If your best work is done away from the home,
you need a new job.
When you work for the Tao
you get time and a half.

25

Before the Universe was born,
there was something mysterious yet absolute,
tranquil and empty,
boundless and constant,
endless and ever-present.
This is what gave birth to the Universe.
It has been called the Tao.

The Tao's most powerful creation is love.
The Tao and its power
flow through everything,
returning to everything.

The Tao is great,
the Universe is great,
Earth is great,
Children are great.
These are the four great powers.

Children love their parents.
Humans love the earth.
The Earth loves the Universe.
The Universe loves the Tao.
The Tao created it all.

26

The Wise Daddy loves arriving home.
It might be messy,
chores to do,
bills to pay,
plans to make,
projects to be done.
He embraces it all,
wholeheartedly.

If you can't embrace your home
and skitter about avoiding duty,
you'll lose touch with your root.

If you are half-hearted in your commitment,
you lose touch with who you are.
Commit to growing
and bear the fruit.

27

The Wise Daddy drives and picks up,
He is kind,
creates fun.
He makes plans but remains open.
The Wise Daddy is friendly
to all Kids.
He rejects no Kid.
He cares for all
using every circumstance to its potential,
wasting nothing.

What is a Good Daddy but a Bad Daddy's teacher?
What is a Bad Daddy but a Good Daddy's job?
It is easier to understand than you think.
It is worth practicing.
This is the great secret.
Now get to it.

28

Respect the power of femininity,
allow it to be a part of your understanding.
If you trust it fully,
the Tao will never leave you.

Teach your Kid the power of femininity,
the courage of masculinity.
Show them when
these opposite forces spin as one,
a higher power is created,
some call it consciousness.

Femininity and masculinity
empower each other.
they both live within us,
part of the primal identity.
The more we accept the other
the more luminous we become,
allowing us to
truly respect the opposite.

Relying on the primal self
is the way.

29

What's the best way to
improve your Daddying?
Accountability, consistency.
Daddying is sacred.
You'll be sorry if you fake it.
Don't blow
the greatest opportunity
in life.

There's a time to win,
a time to lose;
a time to run,
a time to be still;
a time to go crazy,
a time to be tired;
a time to play it safe,
a time to bet big.

The Wise Daddy knows
the world is forever out of control.
He keeps his knees bent
and strives
for balance.

30

Being overbearing goes against the Tao.
Screaming at your Kid
will come back to haunt you.
Hitting your Kid is wrong
and you know it.
The Wise Daddy knows
a Kid must push the limit,
question authority,
go completely nuts.
That's their job.

It's the Wise Daddy's job to be cool,
convince, negotiate.
He knows when to stop talking
and when the action should start.
When the Wise Daddy is connected
His Kid knows how to think,
figure out what to do.
That's the job--
create thinkers and doers.

31

Weapons bring violence,
they are not toys.
Weapons are built to kill.
Period.
A Wise Daddy avoids them.
Using them only in the direst necessity.
Teach reasoning over force,
peace over hate.
Reasoning and peace
are the weapons of the Wise Daddy,
to be used against all enemies.

If forced, and as last resort,
one should fight,
protecting oneself
while using the utmost restraint.

32

The Tao is incomprehensible,
smaller than a grain of sand,
yet contains absolutely everything.
When the Tao is a member of the family,
the family is whole,
the home becomes a sanctuary,
a world unto itself.

In a sanctuary,
too many regulations are dangerous.
Our demands need limits.
Knowing these limits
keeps the Wise Daddy
in charge
of the Kid
and of Himself.

33

Watching others parent is smart,
watching your own parenting is
smarter.
Taking advice can help,
practicing your own advice
is action.

When the family lives in the Tao,
they live beyond
life and death.

34

A Wise Daddy is his parenting,
He pours it into his kid
like honey into tea.
When he trusts the Tao,
he doesn't make claims.
He simply provides
all he can.
His effort vanishes into action,
This is what his Kid calls fun.

To the Kid, fun equals greatness.
True greatness is humble.
The Tao makes it so.

35

Secure in the Tao, the Wise Daddy
takes his Kid everywhere,
and shows them everything,
the good and the bad.
With a heart full of love,
He teaches
you can go where you please,
near and far,
high and low.

Go where you wish --
the Tao is there.

36

You can speak for them
for only so long.
The job is:
Teach them to speak for themselves.
Explain why some words are unacceptable.
A virtuous vocabulary
is worth striving for.
One word at a time.

Let words rain down,
the right ones will nurture,
the wrong will evaporate.
The result will be
the stories they tell.

37

The Wise Daddy is ready.
Ready is the Wise Daddy.
When we give over to the Tao,
our world transforms.
We harmonize with the flow.
Our duty is simple,
our actions fair.

We reject greed
and its trappings.
Free from greed
makes room
For more love

38

Wise Daddies don't try to be good,
they just are.
When the stressed Daddy tries to be good,
he falls short.
Stress envies goodness.

Wise Daddies are at ease, always ready.
The stressed Daddy rushes,
which causes more rushing.
The only thing worse than a stressed Daddy
is a bossy Daddy who abuses his power.
Worse yet: a lazy Daddy
who misses out on the fun.
Worst of all: the mean Daddy.
Mean Daddy's are dangerous,
they create bullies.

If you don't make time,
if you make no effort to improve,
if you are unable to communicate,
scared to love,
friends with hate,
makes you out of balance.

☯

Bullies create bullies.

I suggest you start
looking for the Tao.

The Wise Daddy fears nothing.
He works from deep inside,
encouraging his heart to pump love.
His will is the Tao,
he lives in reality.

39

The Wise Daddy harmonizes the family
with the Tao.
Allowing this,
things stay clean, fresh.
Everyone strives to get along,
constantly helping,
endlessly renewed.

Families caught up in greed
leave a mess wherever they go.
They have little fun
and can't wait to get away from each another.

The Wise Daddy sees it all,
through empathetic eyes,
it all makes sense to him,
even the hardest parts.
He loves his humbleness,
grows old with the Tao.
He keeps it simple and honest,
ordinary
as the day is long.

40

The Wise Daddy gives back,
helping at every turn.
Sure,
there's a million things to do,
each can start with the Tao.

41

When the Wise Daddy first hears the Tao,
there's a déjà vu.
When an average Daddy hears the Tao,
he half believes half doubts.
When a lazy Daddy hears the Tao,
he bursts out laughing.
If he didn't laugh,
it wouldn't be the Tao.

The Wise Daddy realizes:
when Kids get cranky,
they're either tired, hungry,
and or overwhelmed.

A tantrum is a necessary release,
he doesn't hold it against them
he waits, patiently,
for it to blow over.

He monitors the sugar
knowing it's allure
and power.

☯

He knows the tipping point and is
ready to soothe
when stimulation
causes an overload.

The Wise Daddy loves his kid,
regardless.

He understands
they can make him crazy mad,
and when can't solve the puzzle
he consciously changes
his approach.

When starting with humility and
ending in the Tao,
anything can be realized.

42

The Tao gave birth to the universe.
Their Mother gave birth to your Kid.
The burdens are shared,
birthing is not.
The Wise Daddy marvels at the birth.
It inspires him to create marvels himself.
Mommy's marvel
at harmony.

Being a Wise Daddy gets lonely,
he uses it to his advantage,
delving into his aloneness,
knowing the Tao is there
and always will be.

43

Watching the birth,
life starts over.
Once they arrive
it's impossible to believe
that they were once not here.
Ready for responsibility,
set for duty,
the Wise Daddy knows the way.

44

Fantasy or reality: which is more important?
Wealth or health: which is more valuable?
Neglect or overindulgence: which is more destructive?
You don't need to convince others.
Wise Daddies convince only themselves.

If your Kid's desire for stuff is their happiness,
they will never be happy.
Teach them to be happy
with what they have.
When they realize they have enough,
they will be truly rich.
When the child craves things
more than love,
you have work to do.

Happy comes from how it's done.
When you manifest this,
you can make the whole world happy.

45

Even when things go smoothly,
there's always tomorrow.
Even when they laugh,
tears aren't far behind.
Some days are hard.
Some days are very hard.
Some days are very very hard.

The Wise Daddy watches,
he knows.
Time is his friend.
Letting them figure it out,
ready if needed,
yet confident
they can do it
all on their own.

46

When the family denies the Tao,
nightmares can turn into reality.
When a family harmonizes with the Tao,
nightmares are part of our story.

The Wise Daddy doesn't run from fear,
he stands firm.
He explains:
Fear is the great reminder.
We must work to
control and discipline emotions
or they will control and discipline us.
This is fear's purpose.

Practicing control and discipline
over emotions
keeps us further away from panic
and closer to the Tao.

47

Without leaving home,
you can show your Kid the world.
With what's available,
you can practice the Tao.
The less you force,
the easier it becomes.

The Wise Daddy is there,
smile on his face,
ready to help.
He is complete.

48

With other methods,
things are added.
When the Tao is the method,
things are dropped.
Kids do better with less—
less things, less mess.
All the way around.

By shaping the experience
with Nature in mind,
it's easier to find the flow.
The Wise Daddy achieves serenity
not by interfering
but by letting the Tao
simply happen.

49

The Wise Daddy's mind
revolves around his Kid.
The Wise Daddy is kind to his own mind,
kinder still
toward his Kid's mind.

Teaching them to trust their mind,
they learn to trust
the world.
Plant the seed
and one day they will show
their own Kid the Tao.
And being a Grandparent
is supposedly a breeze.

50

The Wise Daddy knows
the value of sleep.
He sings the lullabies,
knowing consciousness relies on sleep
as sleep relies on consciousness.

He plays hard
so they will sleep hard,
knowing that
awake and sleep
spin in an endless cycle,
dreaming, living,
living, dreaming.
Day and night,
night and day,
until the last breath.

51

Open your eyes
it's easy to see,
It's everywhere.
The Tao provides,
helps,
nourishes
and loves.
It reminds us of our purpose:
to provide,
help,
nourish,
and love.

The Tao is instinctual, primal,
ever present.
The Tao guides us,
we guide the Kid.

52

It begins at birth.
Understanding children,
even tiny babies, is within us
when we allow ourselves to remember.

Instinct is the first language.
If you trust only intelligence
and the advice of others,
you force your Kid to learn a foreign language.

Find your native tongue,
have faith in your primal instinct,
recall the language of your youth.
They will return you
to the primal.
This is called living the Tao.

53

When society raises the Kid,
the Kid becomes ward of the state.
When TV becomes the Kid's imagination,
we've wasted a good imagination.
When institutions discipline the Kid,
the parent is not the true parent.
If your Kid doesn't understand greed,
you're in big trouble.

All this is hypnoses and brainwashing,
the antithesis of the Tao.

The Tao is easy, calm and cool.
Let it in
and you will stand sturdy, straight,
balanced and centered.
Leaning toward the sun,
the Tao are the roots.

54

Plant the Tao,
watch it grow.
Live the Tao,
reap the harvest.
Passing it on,
you'll be lovingly remembered.

When you allow the Tao,
you become authentic.
When you're authentic,
you flourish.
When you flourish,
your family flourishes.
When your family flourishes,
they become an example
for the world.
Thrive as a family,
the Universe thrives.

Don't believe me
Look inside.

55

Raising a Kid in the Tao
you'll remember
the joy and power of childhood,
when you were fearless—
eager
to be outside,
intertwined with Nature.
Playing,
Learning,
Laughing.
Your vital energy pulsating
in harmony with your primal being.

The Wise Daddy remembers.
He's excited each day.
This is why
his soul
never grows old.

56

Cheap advice is cheap.
The best advice:
Let them play in nature.
Stand back,
say less,
watch them
connect
with the primal.
Playing in nature
allows the universe in.

It's the answer
to everything.

57

The Wise Daddy leads
by following the Tao.
He has stopped trying to control
what can't be controlled.
Teaching his Kids to handle their business
is his ultimate goal.

The more rules you enforce,
the less original your Kid will be.
The more discipline you demand,
the less flexible they'll be.
If you yell,
don't be surprised
when they yell back.
The only yelling should be cheering.

The Wise Daddy practices
less rules
more cooperation.
If you discipline with love,
they love discipline.
Trust yourself, your Kid, and the Tao.
By following
you will lead.

58

Radiate calm,
Kids understand.
Boiling over,
freaks them out.
Demanding happy
sets up sad.
Demanding good,
sets up bad.
Being bossy
makes it feel like a job.
Nobody likes being bossed
around.

Live your examples.
Keep it simple, precise.
Coating it with humor
makes it easier to remember.
The more you smile,
the more smiles there'll be.

59

The Wise Daddy banks on moderation.
His investment pays
when his Kid shares
and takes pleasure in sharing,
when his Kid works
and loves to earn,
when his Kid has enough
and understands what enough is.

The best part of moderation is
the well-earned splurge.

60

Getting angry happens,
to all of us.
If you allow anger to stay
it's your fault.

Center your Daddying in the Tao,
and anger won't have a chance.
Not that it won't show up
but when it does,
you'll know what to do.
Give it nothing to fight,
anger will vanish
all on its own.

61

The Wise Daddy is responsible with his power.
The more the Kid trusts
this power
the more humility
the Wise Daddy needs.

The Wise Daddy knows his community.
When he makes a mistake,
he isn't afraid to admit it.
He takes pride in correcting it,
thanking those who helped point it out.
He's comfortable
with being uncomfortable.
He strives to have no enemies.

When a community is centered in the Tao,
caring for each and every person
as much as the whole,
other communities will be inspired
to find out
about the Tao.

62

The Tao created the universe.
It is a Wise Daddy's magic,
a bad Daddy's shelter.

Showing off means you're needy.
Let the Tao fill your needs.
The Wise Daddy, like the Tao,
stays humble--
both are content to be mysterious.

When the Wise Daddy sees
a new Daddy in need,
he doesn't bother with small talk.
Instead, he offers
to show him the Tao,
by living it.

When you are one with the Tao,
giving over to the mystery,
people will be drawn to you,
because who doesn't love
a little mystery?

63

Baby steps.
Keep it simple,
steady.
Solve problems
before they're problems.
Consistency is the best way
to accomplish the big goal.

The Wise Daddy is excited
to get the work done.
Work finished equals play time.
He doesn't worry about getting dirty,
He knows how to do laundry.

64

When they're small
they're easier to hold.
Feed them health,
they grow up healthy.
Teach as it's happening,
they become smart.
When they are tired,
get them to sleep.
Take care of business.
Planning for tomorrow
helps today.

Watch carefully,
you can see them grow.
Help them walk
then watch them run.
There is no need to rush,
no need to hold so tight.
Treasure the time.
The clock is ticking,
hear it?

☯

The Wise Daddy takes action
by letting the Kid be,
encouraging freedom.
He gives gifts,
knowing the ultimate gift is his love.
His hope is that one day
his Kid will care for the Tao
so she can help to
care for all things.

65

The Wise Daddy understands that
governments, institutions, and schools
have limitations.
Knowing this
he teaches his Kid
the power and joy of wisdom.

Intelligence has a life span
Wisdom lives forever.

Fancy degrees have their value
but are competitive by nature.
The Wise Daddy teaches
Nature,
which is the Tao.

Content to trust,
following our instincts,
allows us to live simply.
Living simply
reveals our instinct.

Your instinct connects you to the universe.
The universe connects you to the Tao.

66

Humbled by it,
the Wise Daddy commits to his
responsibility.
If you want to raise a wise Kid
you must put yourself below them.
If you want to lead your Kid
you must learn to follow them.

The Wise Daddy stays clam,
no one feels oppressed.
He leads by following
and no one feels left behind.
Everyone is grateful to the Wise Daddy.
He competes with no one
so no one competes with him.

67

Some say the Tao is aloof and unrealistic.
But to those who live it,
the Tao is as real as it gets.

These are the three treasures
of the Tao.
Thus the three treasures
of Wise Daddying:
simplicity, patience, and compassion.
It grows outward from there.

Simple in action and thought
allows contentment.
Patient with both Kids and adults
allows things to unfold naturally.
Compassionate with others and himself,
allows the Wise Daddy to smile,
when he smiles
he harmonizes
with his reality.

68

The best team
wants to play the best teams.
The best players
enter the mind of their opponents.
The best coach believes:
experience first, winning second.
To compete in the spirit of the game is
fun,
especially for the winner.

Kids learn more
from noncompetitive play
than competitive play.
When they are free to be free
their character grows.
And growing character
is more valuable
than winning and losing.

The Tao is noncompetitive,
and is as valuable
as you make it

69

Wise Daddies know:
Bullies are traumatized Kids
hiding behind meanness.
Expose this,
help them to see their fear.
This is called
fighting back by helping.

There is nothing worse
then your Kid falling into the bully trap,
unless your Kid is the bully.

Helping bullies is tough,
but must be done.

70

The Tao makes sense
yet your mind will never fully comprehend it.
Don't over think it
Just allow it.

There is trying
and there is being,
the Wise Daddy knows the difference
by how his Kids respond to him.
Kids don't try to be Kids,
they just are.
Don't *try* to be Wise
just be.
Know the Tao
know your Kid

71

The Wise Daddy knows to
trust the mystery,
to love the mystery,
to praise the mystery.

Knowledge is essential,
but knowledge alone is lonely
when there's living to be done.
The Wise Daddy is his own teacher.
He uses knowledge
but lives the Tao.

72

☯

When their Kid is in trouble
the desperate Daddy panics,
and loses his balance.
Scared, he looks to others for solutions.
Some turn to religion,
or worse allow the TV to sedate
the issue.
When Kids no longer trusts their reality
they lose *their* balance.
When both Daddy and Kid
are out of balance,
bad things happen.

At this point,

The Wise Daddy is already outside,
luring his Kid back into Nature,
allowing the mystery
to do its job.

73

The Wise Daddy
thrives without competing,
answers with action.
He's available,
ready to help,
even when help is not needed.

The Wise Daddy's arms are strong--
they hold the love
he's nurtured into existence.
He cradles it all
right next to his heart.
Ready to set it free
When the time is right.

74

The Wise Daddy knows change,
he lives for it.
Not afraid to love,
he loves his Kid wholeheartedly.
This is the only thing
that doesn't change.
This love
lives for eternity.

The average Daddy loves lazily:
"Do as I say, not as I do."
Eventually, his laziness
becomes their laziness,
and the average Daddy becomes
mad.
At whom, though?

75

Don't tend your garden,
no harvest.
Your love is their fertilizer.
The Tao
their sun.

There's only so much
tending to do.
You must let them be,
to ripen
properly.

76

The Wise Daddy is alert, alive.
Other Daddies are lost, desperate.
The lost and desperate
spin in misery.
Those that stay alert,
stay alive.

While other Daddies wallow,
Wise Daddies flourish.

The Wise Daddy
strives for balance.
He is ready to help
or be helped,
giving
receiving,
balanced.

Kids learn from watching.

So a Wise Daddy's Kid knows,
needed or not,
they help.
And Just as important,
when they need help
they ask for help.

78

Water is soft and comforting,
yet cleans the dirty.
Nothing calms a Kid like a warm bath.
The soft overcomes the hard,
the calm overcomes the panicked.
Everyone understands this,
the Wise Daddy lives this.

The Wise Daddy isn't scared to be
vulnerable.
Summoning his courage
he walks the tightrope,
step by step.
His safety net is the Tao.

79

The Wise Daddy isn't afraid to fail.
He doesn't waste time with blame.
Accountability is the skeleton of his identity.
He takes care of business,
cleans up his messes,
plans for the future,
while relishing the moment.

In that moment,
he dances with the Tao.

80

When the Wise Daddy is on,
the family is happy.
They have fun
within themselves.
They love their home,
take pride in what happens there.
Sometimes they travel,
Yet love being home
talking,
playing,
dancing,
creating,
cooking,
eating.
The love and care of the home
mean everything to the family.

They know the neighbors
and the neighborhood,
but inside the home
is where the magic
and the mystery live.

81

The Wise Daddy knows
he can't explain the Tao.
He chooses instead
to live it.

By being himself,
embracing his duty,
he's ready for the Kid
to balance and enrich his life.

By embracing the mystery,
with nature as his guide,
the Wise Daddy
walks his path
wide-eyed,
hand in hand
with his Kid
immersed in the Tao,
anticipating those precious words,
"I love you Daddy."